GEORG

# PERUVIAN POTTERY

SHIRE ETHNOGRAPHY

2

*Cover photograph*
Spout and handle bottle depicting a person, probably a shaman or witch-doctor,
wearing a pampas cat (*Felis colocolo*) skin headdress and holding a snake.
(Nasca, phase 1; height 205 mm. Manchester Museum, 0.9707/55.)

British Library Cataloguing in Publication Data:
Bankes, George, 1945-.
Peruvian Pottery. (Shire ethnography: 15.)
1. History, Peruvian, pottery.
I. Title.
738.3'0985.
ISBN 0-7478-0013-8.

Published by
SHIRE PUBLICATIONS LTD
Cromwell House, Church Street, Princes Risborough,
Aylesbury, Bucks HP17 9AJ, UK.

Series Editor: Bryan Cranstone.

ISBN 0 7478 0013 8.

First published 1989.

Printed in Great Britain by C. I. Thomas & Sons (Haverfordwest) Ltd,
Press Buildings, Merlins Bridge, Haverfordwest, Dyfed SA61 1XF.

# Contents

# Acknowledgements

I wish to express my thanks to Yoshio Onuki of Tokyo University, Dr Frank Norick of the Lowie Museum, Berkeley, Dale Idiens and Margaret Watson of the Royal Museum of Scotland, Edinburgh, and Mrs A. B. Isaac and Dr Rosemary Joyce of the Peabody Museum, Harvard University, for assistance in supplying photographs and granting permission for their reproduction in this book. I am grateful also to Dr Walter Alva for allowing me to reproduce items from the Brüning Museum, Lambayeque. Mrs Hepzibah Yohannan prepared the line drawings. Finally I am most indebted to Wilf Thomas, Cathy Street-Cunningham and Pat Tapping for photographing the Manchester Museum pottery and to Carole Higginbottom for typing the original manuscript.

4

# List of illustrations

## CHRONOLOGY

| Period | Date | Culture/area |
| --- | --- | --- |
| Late Horizon | AD 1476-1532 | Inca |
| Late Intermediate Period | AD 900-1476 | Chimu<br>Chancay |
| Middle Horizon | AD 600-900 | Wari<br>Tiwanaku |
| Early Intermediate Period | 300 BC-AD 600 | Moche<br>Nasca<br>Recuay<br>Gallinazo<br>Salinar |
| Early Horizon | 1000-300 BC | Paracas<br>Cupisnique<br>Chavín |
| Initial Period | 1800-1000 BC | Ancón<br>Guañape<br>Kotosh |
| Earliest pottery | *c.*3000-1800 BC | Tutishcainyo<br>Central Ucayali |

**1.** Map of Peru showing the physical features, archaeological sites and towns mentioned in the text.

# 1
# Peru and her people

## Environment

The modern republic of Peru is located on the west coast of South America, mostly between latitudes 4 and 18 degrees south. It covers a huge area, over 496,000 square miles (1,050,000 square km), which is five times the size of the British Isles. The area generally considered as pre-Hispanic (before AD 1532) Peru is usually only the coast and highlands, including the part of the Bolivian uplands round Lake Titicaca. The environment of modern Peru varies considerably from a coastal desert on the west through mountains with a snow line to dense tropical forest in the Upper Amazon in the east.

Most of the coast is a desert, which is in places 50 miles (80 km) wide, while elsewhere the mountains come right to the sea. There are extensive stretches of sand dunes in many areas while in others there are rock deserts of boulders and small stones. There is little precipitation over much of the coast apart from sea fogs. These result from cool air above the Humboldt Current, an upwelling of cold water from the ocean off the coast of Peru, moving over the warm land. These fogs are mainly over the central and north coasts from about May to October. Periodically warm waters called *El Niño* (Spanish for 'the child') push southwards off Ecuador. This leads to a rise in temperature and causes quite heavy rainfall on the coast. When this happened in March and April 1983, Piura received about 5 feet (150 cm) of rain in one night. This seriously affected the potters of Simbilá, near Piura, and Morrope, near Chiclayo, who were unable to produce any ceramics for months because of flooding and general dampness. There is evidence of similar heavy rains in antiquity on the north coast, such as in the Trujillo area where sections of some irrigation canals were washed away.

In general, the temperature along the coast of Peru does not have great daily or annual fluctuations. Between October and May there is usually plenty of sunshine, which is very important for drying and firing pottery.

The coastal desert is crossed by many short rivers, mainly seasonal in flow. The smaller ones run dry or have a reduced flow from May to November but the larger ones, mainly on the north coast, flow all year round. In antiquity these valleys were well wooded with trees like *algarrobo* and *zapote*, both of which are used today by potters as fuel for firing. Irrigation agriculture was widely practised in antiquity as it is today. In pre-Hispanic times communication between these coastal valleys was not easy since between them there are rocky spurs and large areas of sand hills. Therefore each tended to have its own cultural identity and this is reflected in the pottery styles.

The Peruvian highlands are part of the Andean chain that runs down the west side of South America. The Peruvian Andes are high, the highest over 21,655 feet (6600 metres), and rugged with little vegetation on the western slopes. In pre-Hispanic times there were about six areas that supported substantial populations and these included the basins round Cajamarca, Ayacucho and Cuzco and the Bolivian plateau south of Lake Titicaca. Even today parts of these areas are still quite densely populated. Communications between the highlands and coast are mainly through the river valleys and this has facilitated cultural influences and trade from earliest times.

The climate in the mountains has two main seasons: a rainy one from December to March and a dry one for the rest of the year. Occasionally the rains begin in November and last into April. This means that in the highlands the best time for making pottery is from April to October since there is sunshine for drying.

The eastern slopes of the Andes, where rain falls from westward winds, is a heavily forested transitional zone called the *montaña*. At the foot of these slopes lies the Upper Amazon Basin. This area is crossed by slow meandering rivers and streams which often change course. The thick vegetation cover includes some economically important trees such as those in the genera *Protium* and *Hymenea*, which produce the resin used to glaze much of the Upper Amazon pottery. These trees were, and are, quite widely distributed so that, between tribes and villages a long way apart, it was necessary to trade mainly via the waterways.

**People**
The original inhabitants of Peru were American Indians whose ancestors migrated from north-west Asia via North and Central America over fifteen thousand years ago. The physical features of their descendants include some Asian characteristics such as an internal epicanthic fold giving a 'slant' eyed appearance, dark eyes and straight black hair. The ancient Peruvian Indians were, like their descendants today, short and stocky with short, medium to broad heads, fairly short faces and moderately broad noses. In spite of their Asiatic ancestry quite a range of racial characteristics does appear in ancient pottery, especially that of the Moche,

**2.** (Left) Bottle with traces of resin on the neck and chamber. From the montaña on the west side of the Upper Amazon. Probably made *c.*1850-1900. Height 280 mm. (Manchester Museum, 0.9707/54.)

**3.** (Right) Moche IV portrait head of a person with an internal epicanthic fold, *c.*400-600; height 180 mm. (Manchester Museum, 0.9707/31.)

so that sometimes marked negroid elements are shown. These differences were probably the result of natural genetic variations within the population.

There were some physical adaptations according to altitude. The thin air of the highlands, with little oxygen, led to the development of large lungs in deep barrel chests. Some pre-Hispanic pottery shows people with deformed heads; this is the result of deformation carried out intentionally on Indian children. It was probably done by applying pressure with boards and straps when the baby was asleep so that when it grew up the infant would have a flattened forehead or an elongated head.

When the Spaniards discovered Peru in the fifteenth century the official language of the Inca empire was Quechua. Quechua is now the second official language after Spanish and is quite widely used in the central and southern highlands. Spanish is commonly used and the majority of the terms used to describe pottery and its manufacture, particularly on the coast, are in that language.

The modern population of Peru is concentrated on the coast in large cities like Lima and Trujillo, although since the early 1980s there has been some movement away from Lima. The population contains European elements from Spanish and later European immigration but the American Indian physique is still very widespread. One reason for this is that when the Spaniards conquered Peru they initially brought no women with them and took Indian wives. While there is a strong Hispanic element in Peruvian culture, especially in urban environments, pre-Hispanic influences are present. The past has been used to promote national identity and ancient pots have appeared on postage stamps. Within Indian communities in the highlands and in some of the coastal villages indigenous cultural elements like the practice of reciprocity are found. The Inca state was built on a pattern of reciprocity whereby protection and much *chicha* (maize beer) was provided in return for labour on state projects. Now it is more a pattern of returning favours, such as helping a relative or neighbour work his land, and this assistance will be returned at a later date. Much *chicha* is drunk at certain festivals and parties. Many pots were needed to make, store and serve the *chicha* and still are in certain parts of the country.

**4.** *Taberna* or set of six *ollas* set in the ground. Fuel is placed round each pot, inside which a mixture of maize flour and water is boiled to make *chicha*. Simbilá, 1984. (Photograph: George Bankes.)

# 2
# Chronology of Peruvian pottery

**Earliest pottery**

The earliest pottery in South America has been found on the coast of Ecuador and Colombia and also near the mouth of the river Amazon. Relatively simple pottery was being made by 3000 BC at Valdivia on the south coast of Ecuador and at Puerto Hormiga on the Caribbean coast of Colombia. According to work carried out by Brochado, a Brazilian archaeologist, simple shell-tempered pottery, globular in shape, from several sites near the mouth of the Amazon, has been securely dated at earlier than 3100 BC. Sherds of similar simple shell-tempered ware have been found by Donald Lathrap, a North American archaeologist, in the area of the Central Ucayali river in the Upper Amazon in Peru. Lathrap has dated this shell-tempered pottery at 3000 BC but this date is not accepted by all the other archaeologists who work in Peru.

This early shell-tempered ware was itself ground up for temper to make a pottery style termed Early Tutishcainyo by Lathrap and found just north-west of the modern town of Pucallpa. The date for this culture is about 2000 BC. The site where this pottery was found is just an alluvial hillock with a rubbish heap on top containing a lot of pottery. The most common form was a large wide-mouthed bowl with a flanged lip, round base and concave sides. Lathrap reckoned the size and shape of this bowl meant that it was used for cooking. Bowls with shorter sides probably served as plates for solid foods. In addition there were smaller vessels with inward-sloping sides that could have held drinks like gruel or beer. One rare form was a double spout and bridge bottle consisting of two spouts joined by a curved bridge, which would have been quite difficult to make. This shape also occurs in the earliest pottery on the coast of Peru.

There are conflicting opinions as to whether or not pottery was invented indigenously in Peru. Catherine Rozenberg, a Peruvian archaeologist, maintains that it was. She sees it as a casual invention, citing fieldwork at Piruru on the upper Marañon river, about 50 miles (80 km) north-west of Kotosh. At Piruru the cremation of offerings at a temple led to the firing of the clay used to line the offering chamber, dating to between 2500 and 1900 BC. In her view the earliest pottery from the Peruvian Andes comes from the central and northern Andes and dates to the first

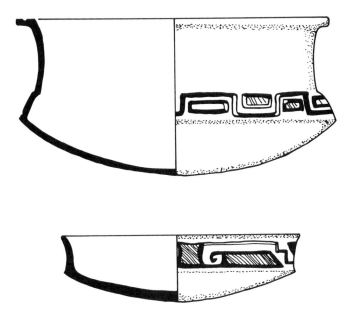

**5.** Two Early Tutishcainyo vessel forms. The most common (above) was a large open-mouthed bowl with concave sides, flanged lip and incised decoration, probably used for cooking. The broad open bowl (below) could have been a plate for solid foods. (After Lathrap, Donald R., *The Upper Amazon*, figures 7b and 7f.)

half of the second millennium BC. In contrast, the earliest pottery in the Zaña Valley, about 80 miles (50 km) south-east of Chiclayo, has been dated to 2500 to 1800 BC and related to the Middle and Late Valdivia Phases, according to work by Thomas Dillehay and other North American archaeologists. Pottery similar to Valdivia wares has also been found in the Piura and Jequetepeque valleys. This evidence suggests the technique of making pottery may have spread to the north coast of Peru from Ecuador. Indigenous highland inventions as at Piruru also probably occurred.

**Ceramics in pre-Hispanic Peru**

The invention of pottery does not seem to have had any significant economic impact on Peru, especially since agriculture had already been in existence on both coast and highlands for a thousand years. Decorated wares, along with a few utility vessels, were placed in tombs, indicating the status of the deceased. Decorated vessels reflected social and religious developments as well as cultural influences. The chronology of pre-Hispanic Peru after the introduction of pottery has largely been reconstructed on changes in decorated ceramic styles by working backwards from the Inca conquest.

This chronological scheme has produced three periods of unification or 'horizons' and three 'intermediate periods' of regional cultures. Working backwards, there is the Late Horizon (Inca Empire) from about AD 1476 to 1532. Before this, from about AD 900 to 1476, is the Late Intermediate Period, a time of regional states. This succeeds another period of some unification, based on Wari and Tiwanaku, termed the Middle Horizon, between about AD 600 and 900. Before this was another period of regionalism characterised by pottery of high artistic quality, especially of the Moche and Nasca styles, termed the Early Intermediate Period, from about 300 BC to AD 600. This succeeded the Early Horizon, a period of religious centres culminating in influence from the temple of Chavín de Huántar, which ran from about 1000 BC to 300 BC. Finally there is the Initial Period from about 1800 BC to 1000 BC when the first pottery was made in the highlands and on the coast.

### Initial Period

At the temple site of Kotosh, in the Huanuco area, three phases of pottery have been recognised. The earliest, termed Waira-jirca, has been dated to 1800 BC. For the first time stirrup spout shapes, consisting of a chamber with a stirrup-shaped handle set on the top or side, appear in the Central Andes but the main ones are open forms that resemble cups and vases. The diagnostic type of decoration consists of bands of fine parallel

**6.** Two Waira-jirca phase vessels from Kotosh (*c.*1800 BC): (left) bowl with post-fired polychrome painting in incised lines, diameter 216 mm; (right) bowl with incised hachure in incised zones, diameter 156 mm. (Courtesy of Yoshio Onuki and University of Tokyo Expedition.)

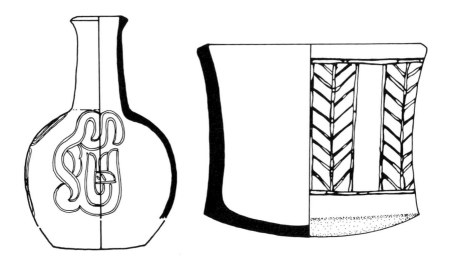

7. (Left) Reconstructed polished blackware bottle from Chavín de Huántar with four stylised incised felines set vertically on the chamber; height 196 mm. (After Lambreras, Luis G., 'Excavaviones en el Templo Antiguo de Chavín (Sector R); Informe de la Sexta Campaña', in *Ñawpa Pacha 15*, figure 15a.)

8. (Right) Urabarriu-phase cup from Chavín de Huántar with an incised fern design, *c*. 860-460 BC; height 67 mm. (After Burger, Richard L., *The Prehistoric Occupation of Chavín de Huántar, Peru*, figure 25.)

lines filled with red, white or yellow pigment after firing. Another method of decoration was excision, in which part of the surface was removed to produce differences in elevation. Waira-jirca is too sophisticated to be considered an initial style and it is most likely that it developed from earlier tropical forest styles like Early Tutishcainyo.

On the central coast pottery appears well made by about 1800 BC. Here a pottery sequence of at least seven phases has been identified on the coast between Ancón and Lima. Designs on Ancón ceramics were done by incision, punctation and painting. On the south coast initial pottery dates are between 1297 and 997 BC. The most unusual characteristic of this south coast pottery is negative painting, a technique that produced contrasting tones by covering up designs with clay or some similar substance that can be removed after firing. This technique became much more common later in the first millennium BC.

On the north coast Initial Period pottery has been identified in the Virú and Moche valleys. In Moche the most common pottery was a thick oxidised ware with a lot of coarse river sand and temper. In Virú it was mainly plain and dark reddish-brown or black. Vessel shapes consisted of jars with round bases with either a short neck or none at all. Decoration was simple and included fingertip impressions, punctation and incisions on appliqué ribs. As was the case with the highlands, this coastal pottery is too sophisticated to represent a developmental stage and so its origins may be in Ecuador.

In the Initial Period elaborate ceremonial constructions were erected on the coast, and in the highlands. Permanent settlements increased in size and number, especially on the coast, where seafood provided an important element in the diet.

**Early Horizon**

The best known Early Horizon pottery styles are those connected with Chavín de Huántar and the spread of its influence to the north coast from 800 to 600 BC. Chavín de Huántar is a temple which was originally started about 1000 BC and continued in use for about seven hundred years. Its art is complex and the most complete examples are found in stone carvings of anthropomorphic beings, felines, birds of prey and caymans. The site lies at over 9800 feet (3000 metres) in the Mosna Valley, whose river joins the Marañon, a tributary of the Amazon. This is significant since many of the fauna shown in Chavín art are from the tropical forest.

The fine pottery of Chavín is noted for its plastic techniques of decoration. The earliest phase, termed Urabarriu, from about 860 to 460 BC, included many bowls, neckless *ollas* (globular-shaped cooking pots) and bottles, including stirrup spouts. These were mainly dark grey and the bottles were decorated by techniques like incision, punctation and rocker stamping, which consisted of rocking a shell backwards and forwards. In addition, differential polishing was used in conjunction with textured surfaces, made up of lines of small depressions formed by shells or combs, to create a contrast between zones demarcated by incision. By the Chakinani phase, from about 460 to 390 BC, stirrup spout bottles had become more important. Incision was the main decorative technique, with the emphasis shifting to complex geometric and iconographic motifs like those found on the stone carvings. Surfaces were better polished, with graphite slip being applied after polishing and decoration, and graphite paint was used together with red slip to produce a contrast in colour. Finally in the Janabarriu phase, from 390 to 200 BC, many fine bowls, including numerous oversize ones covered with a weak red slip, were made. Bottles also continued in stirrup spout and single-spout forms with rims thickened to produce a flange with a broad flat surface at the top of the rim.

The version of Chavín pottery that spread to the north coast is termed Cupisnique after the place where it was first identified. The most common vessels are flat-based stirrup spout bottles. Some have globular chambers while others are modelled in the form of aquatic and terrestrial animals.

On the south coast, the Paracas pottery style developed in the Ica, Nazca and Acari valleys in the second half of the first millennium BC out of Chavín antecedents. Initially Paracas pottery contained some diagnostic Chavín elements like globular stirrup spout bottles with designs like felines outlined by fine line incisions. The areas between the incisions were filled with brightly coloured resin paint in shades of red, orange, yellow, blue, green and brown applied after firing. Negative painting was effected in the form of circles, dots and lines in a lighter slip under a dark over-colour.

Chavín influence took place in the context of settled village and urban life on an agricultural foundation assisted by irrigation. This influence is usually seen in terms of a religion or ideology rather than any political or military empire. By about 200 BC the influence of Chavín had more or less died out over most of Peru.

**Early Intermediate Period**
In the early centuries BC distinctive regional ceramic styles began to emerge, especially along the Peruvian coast. These crystallised in the first half of the first millennium AD into major artistic traditions, especially on the north and south coasts. In the

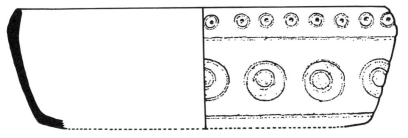

**9.** Janabarriu phase bowl from Chavín de Huántar with incised circles, some with punctate centres, *c*.390-200 BC; height 68 mm. (After Burger, Richard L., *The Prehistoric Occupation of Chavín de Huántar, Peru*, figure 247.)

**10.** (Left) Salinar stirrup spout bottle in the shape of a building, with an incised double snake head, outlined in white slip, on the front. From the Chicama Valley; height 205 mm. (Courtesy of Peabody Museum, Harvard University, 46-77-30/4912. Photograph: Hillel Burger.)

**11.** (Right) Gallinazo double-chambered bottle. The light wavy horizontal lines have been made by negative painting. Said to be from the north coast. Height 135 mm. (Courtesy of Peabody Museum, Harvard University, 47-63-30/5680. Photograph: Hillel Burger.)

north, sculptural form with the use of few colours dominated while in the south complex polychrome designs with little emphasis on relief became the norm. The quantity and quality of the coastal Early Intermediate pottery suggests that it was made by full-time specialists.

*North Coast styles.* Towards the end of Chavín influence on the north coast a red to buff coloured pottery termed Salinar was made in the Chicama, Moche and Virú valleys. The Salinar potters continued the Chavín tradition of a stirrup spout bottle but introduced two new forms: a spout and handle bottle and a figure spout and bridge bottle. The feline motif of Cupisnique disappeared, although incised lines were used to outline white-painted zones. Modelled human and animal forms like those in

Cupisnique continued except that erotic scenes were introduced. Appliqué modelling was combined with incision, and sculptural details were enlivened by painting. Salinar pottery was made between about 500 and 300 BC.

In the Chicama, Moche and Virú valleys Salinar pottery was succeeded by a style termed Gallinazo, which lasted from about 300 BC to AD 200. Many of the Gallinazo shapes were similar to those of Salinar but the modelling was more naturalistic. Negative painting ranging from simple geometric designs to feline figures was widely used, along with incision and punched hole decoration. In addition there was some positive painting in white on red. There was some overlap between the Gallinazo and Moche and Recuay styles so that towards the end of Gallinazo it was influenced most by Moche, such as in shapes like face-neck jars and greater emphasis on modelling.

Although the Recuay culture originated in the highlands in the upper Santa Valley it did exert influence on both Gallinazo and Moche ceramics. Its approximate dates are AD 200 to 600. Recuay pottery is very distinctive with its usually white paste. The main shapes are bowls, dippers, spoons, jars, bottles with modelled heads joined by a bridge to a spout, stirrup spout bottles and figure vessels. Modelled animals or humans singly or in scenes were placed in the upper parts of some vessels. Frequently animals like the jaguar, armadillo, condor, heron and owl are shown. Human depictions included warriors, sometimes with human trophy heads. Both positive and negative techniques

**12.** Pedestal cup. Six felines like that shown are negative painted on a black background on the exterior. From Pashash, Cabana cream ware, Recuay-style; height 700 mm. (After Grieder, Terence, *The Art and Archaeology of Pashash*, figure 10/4.19.)

**13.** (Left) Stirrup spout bottle in the form of a skull with features outlined in orange slip. The stylised modelling and flanged lip typify Moche II. Height 250 mm. (Manchester Museum, 0.9707/12.)

**14.** (Right) Stirrup spout bottle with cream slip decoration on orange. The stirrup spout, handle shape and decoration are typical of Moche III. Height 220 mm. (Manchester Museum, 0.9707/17.)

were used to produce pottery painted in two-colour and three-colour designs in black, white and red. The main motifs were generally a two-headed snake and a feline or dragon with bared teeth.

Overlapping in time with the Recuay and Gallinazo styles is that of the Moche. This began about the beginning of the Christian era in the Moche and Chicama valleys and continued until about AD 700, when its influence extended from Lambayeque in the north to Nepeña in the south, a distance of about 186 miles (300 km). Many scholars see Moche as a unified state with urban centres and extensive irrigation agriculture. However, while there is considerable archaeological evidence for this, the decorated pottery gives an impression of regional variations within this overall pattern. For example, in the Santa Valley, the

**15.** (Left) Stirrup spout bottle with dark red slip painted on cream. The triangular-shaped stirrup handle and tapering spout are typical of Moche V. Height 260 mm. (Manchester Museum, 0.8994/2.)

**16.** (Right) Double spout and bridge bottle depicting a mythical feline, probably derived from the pampas cat (*Felis colocolo*). Painted black, dark red, orange and white. Early Nasca, phase 2; height 135 mm. (Manchester Museum, 0.8129.)

Moche ceramics tend to have a thick white matt slip applied, while in the Viru Valley a significantly greater use was made of a fugitive black paint in addition to the usual shades of red and white found in the Moche and Chicama valleys.

Throughout the Moche decorated style the stirrup spout bottle was a prominent form inherited from Cupisnique. Changes in the shape of the stirrup spout handle, along with the form and content of the iconography, have been seen as marking five phases of the culture as a whole.

Moche I stirrup spout bottles have a pronounced flange on the lip of the spout and the handles are circular. The walls are fairly thick, making the pots heavy. The forms are squat and compact with little suggestion of movement. In phase II the stirrup spout bottles are larger with less thick walls. The stirrup handle is taller, while there is only a vestigial flange on the lip of the spout. The painted lines on Moche II pieces are more refined than on Moche I examples and designs tend to be geometric. In spite of these differences there are overlaps between these phases and pieces are found which are transitional. In addition, relatively smaller quantities of pottery than can be assigned to these first two phases have been found outside the Moche and Chicama valleys.

There was a gradual transition from Moche II to III. In the third phase the amount of pottery increased considerably, as did the number of decorative motifs. The handles and spouts of stirrup spout bottles were considerably refined. Handles were elliptical, while spouts had a short, almost imperceptible flange early in phase III which disappeared later on. Modelled pottery showed more realism than before, while painted scenes became more lively with thinner lines. There was a gradual transition to phase IV when Moche power was at its height. On stirrup spout bottles, spouts were bigger and longer with straight sides and handles were more rounded. There were also many relief heads. Fillers appeared in scenic decoration and the thickness of line was reduced. The fifth and final phase of Moche included a few examples of polychrome decoration derived from ceramic styles associated with the expansion of Wari. The shape of the stirrup handle became almost triangular, while spouts were short and tapering. Very elaborate fine line drawings were executed on some stirrup spout bottles.

*South coast styles.* The most prominent of the south coast styles in the Early Intermediate Period was that of Nasca, whose area of distribution included the valleys of Nazca, Ica, Chincha, Pisco and Acari. Although Nasca pottery has been intensively studied there are two main differing chronologies. Some scholars have divided this style into nine subphases while others have made only three major divisions. Certainly a distinction can be made between early, middle and late Nasca pottery from its beginnings about 300 BC to about AD 600. Modelling is not often found in Nasca ceramics since the emphasis is on polychrome painted designs.

The earliest Nasca pottery includes many features of the preceding Paracas style. The most significant change was the substitution of pre-fired painting for the rather fugitive negative technique. Painted designs in colours such as red, white, black, orange and brown were delimited by very fine incisions. By about AD 100 Nasca pottery became a more refined naturalistic style.

*Peruvian Pottery*

**17.** (Left) Effigy bottle of a person wearing a sleeveless shirt. Late Nasca, phase 6 shape and style of painting; height 180 mm. (Manchester Museum, 0.7918.)

**18.** (Right) Vase with alternating friezes of figures holding plants, including beans and peppers, and with a line of slightly modelled trophy heads round the middle and base. Painted black, white, dark red, orange and grey. Late Nasca, *c.* phase 7; height 235 mm. (Manchester Museum, 0.7907.)

In this early style durable pigments of mineral origin were applied to double spout and bridge bottles, bowls and plates. Up to eight colours were used in multicoloured designs outlined with black lines on red-slipped surfaces. Painted designs consist mainly of a central motif without space fillers.

About AD 300 Nasca pottery seems to have become more abstract with the introduction of ornamental volutes and increasingly the whole surface was covered with designs. The style of this middle phase seems to show an abrupt transformation from the early ceramics. The reason for this could well be foreign influence, possibly from the Ayacucho area, where many middle

**19.** (Left) Polychrome painted figurine in orange, black, dark red, white and purple. The clay pellets inside suggest it was a rattle. The 'tear ducts' running from each eye are probably derived from Wari iconography. Middle Horizon; height 165 mm. (Manchester Museum, 0.9707/60.)

**20.** (Right) Beaker or *kero* painted in black on orange with a conventionalised design including steps, eyes and possibly legs. Tiwanaku phase IV or V, *c.* AD 700-900; height 195 mm. (Manchester Museum, 0.9707/51.)

Nasca traits have been found. Technically Nasca ceramics reached their peak in this period with sophisticated and beautifully polished forms. Up to ten or twelve distinct colours were used. During the fifth century AD the designs on Nasca ceramics became even more convoluted with a proliferation of motifs. The few modelled pieces were almost entirely restricted to human forms. Finally, during the latter part of the sixth century and during the seventh century AD Nasca ceramics declined in quality. Most designs were reduced to abstract volutes. The reason for this was increasing influence from Wari, near Ayacucho.

**Middle Horizon**
    From about AD 600 to 900 Wari, a large urban settlement, and
Tiwanaku, a substantial ceremonial centre, exerted influence in
varying degrees over part of Bolivia and Chile and central and·
southern Peru. Most of the evidence for this has come from
distinctive pottery styles.
    Tiwanaku may well have been a pilgrimage centre for people
from the Ayacucho area. At Conchopata near Ayacucho huge
pottery urns about 75 cm high with sides 7 cm thick have been
found in pits. These are painted in polychrome with mythical
figures holding a staff in each hand very similar to those found on
ceremonial pottery and in stone carving at Tiwanaku. These huge
ceremonial urns were broken in antiquity with a blow to the face
of the figure. After about AD 650 these ceremonial urns with
mythical figures were being made on the south coast at Pacheco
in the upper Nazca valley. By this time Wari had become firmly
established as a major urban centre about 18½ miles (30 km)
north of Ayacucho. Here fragments of huge pottery urns like
those from Conchopata have been found with similar mythical
designs. Most Wari ceramics were secular but gradually elements
of, and finally whole, mythical designs appeared on them,
indicating the secularisation of Wari society. This type of pottery
became the hallmark of Wari influence in southern and central
Peru with some in the north.
    The pottery of Tiwanaku is usually polychrome on an orange
base with frequent depictions, probably derived from religious
stone carvings, of felines, snakes and humans. The most
characteristic shape is the beaker or *kero*, which was diffused
throughout the southern Andes from about AD 500 to 900. By
about the ninth century the unified designs had broken down into
geometric elements, reflecting the declining influence of Tiwanaku.

**Late Intermediate Period**
    After about AD 900 a number of regional styles dominated
Peru until the Inca conquest in the second half of the fifteenth
century. The most productive in terms of pottery was that of the
Chimu, whose empire, at its maximum extent in 1460, extended
from Tumbes in the north to the Huara Valley in the south. Much
of this Late Intermediate pottery seems to have been mass-
produced, making extensive use of press moulding, and most
lacks the artistic quality found in Early Intermediate Period
ceramics.

21. Face-neck bottle painted with a black geometric design. Said to have been found in 1878 near the Huaca del Sol, Trujillo. Early Chimu, *c.* AD 900-1150; height 110 mm. (Manchester Museum, 0.9707/47.)

Early Chimu pottery found in the Moche Valley, made from about AD 900 to 1150, shows some continuity with the Moche tradition, such as press moulding and reduction-fired blackware, but differs in other ways, such as the lack of stirrup spout bottles. There is some evidence of Wari influence in bottles with a bridge handle and a tapering spout and in red, white and black pigments applied before firing. In addition, oxidised redware was made. One new form introduced was a small ring-base bowl. During the middle Chimu period, between about 1150 and 1300, Chan Chan became established as the Chimu capital on the lower north side of the Moche Valley. At this time tripod bowls were common and plates appeared for the first time. Some stirrup spout bottles were reintroduced. Paddle stamping makes its first appearance in the Moche Valley and there is much more burnishing and reduction-fired blackware. In late Chimu times, up to about 1460, mould-made and reduction-fired blackware continued. However, oxidised redwares, particularly utility vessels, were common.

Tripod vessels and ring-base bowls were no longer made. Middle Chimu-type oval blackware jars continued, but now they had an addition in the form of a separately modelled head set just below the neck. Stirrup spout bottles also continued. Finally, with the Inca conquest of the Chimu kingdom in the 1460s, many of the existing forms continued to be made using the same techniques but with some modifications. For example, stirrup spout bottles acquired a pronounced flaring lip. Inca introductions included aryballoid forms and plates with squared rims and angled bases.

The other main Late Intermediate pottery style is that of Chancay, which has been found on the central coast, particularly in the Chancay and Chillón valleys. The most common vessel shapes found in tombs include oblong jars with a narrow neck on which is a modelled and painted human face, jars with a narrow neck and incurving rim with handles running from the neck to the body, and nude, standing, female effigy figures with arms outstretched. The surface is rarely smooth since the clay used was rather gritty. The workmanship is fairly crude with a blackish paint being used on a whitish slip, although sometimes a red pigment was also employed.

**22.** Tripod bowl in redware with remains of a black slip decoration on a cream base. One leg has a small pellet inside it. Middle Chimu, *c.*1150-1300. Height 85 mm. (Manchester Museum, 0.8153.)

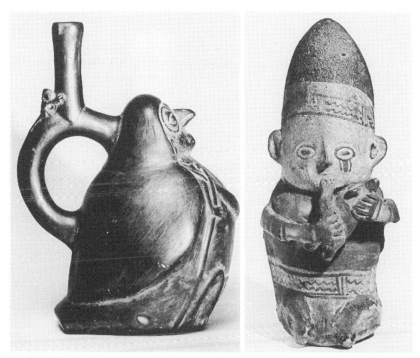

**23.** (Left) Reduction-fired blackware stirrup spout bottle depicting an anthropomorphic figure with a bird's beak and eyes and human hands and feet. The bulging spout with the small monkey at the base is typical of Late Chimu, *c*.1300-1400. Height 250 mm. (Manchester Museum, 0.8994/10.)

**24.** (Right) Figure of a squatting person holding a child, painted black on cream. The 'tears' under each eye probably represent face paint. Chancay, 1200-1460; height 270 mm. (Manchester Museum, 0.9707/53.)

## Late Horizon

By 1476 the Inca empire covered the highlands and coast of modern Peru and by the end of that century it extended from central Chile up to Quito in Ecuador. In ceramic terms there was a Cuzco Inca style and variations on Inca shapes and designs occurred in different parts of the Empire. Cuzco pottery is characterised by geometric designs, usually in black and white, on a red background. The most diagnostic designs are a spreading fern motif and black triangles or rhomboids, usually set in horizontal rows. Modelling is secondary to painted decoration. When naturalistic forms like birds and animals are employed they are often very stylised and conform to an abstract pattern of design. Typical shapes are beakers, shallow round plates and aryballoid jars which have a long narrow neck with a flaring rim and a rounded chamber with two handles and a pointed base. These aryballoid jars were made in both small and large sizes and used for storing liquids. The Cuzco aryballo has a small modelled figure at the base of the neck. Cuzco Imperial pottery has been found throughout the Empire in Inca administrative centres, where it was imported by the governing elite as a status symbol. Since Inca domination of much of Peru lasted only about sixty years the ceramic influence soon disappeared after the Spanish conquest in the 1530s.

**25.** (Left) Aryballoid jar decorated on facing side only in red, white and black on orange. Probably for offerings of liquids. From the north coast, Inca; height 170 mm. (Manchester Museum, 0.8997.)

**26.** (Right) Beaker painted with a Cuzco Imperial-style geometric design. Probably used for drinking *chicha*. Height 125 mm. (Manchester Museum, 0.8994/3.)

# 3
# The technology of pre-Hispanic and modern pottery

The methods used to make and decorate pre-Hispanic pottery in Peru can be partially determined by studying the finished products, although many of the processes of manufacture have often been erased. X-ray analyses and some experiments have been used to determine the processes of manufacture of Moche pottery. In addition, there is a significant number of modern potters, especially on the north coast, who use ancient techniques like paddle and anvil to make their wares. There has also been a revival, starting in the late 1970s, of the ancient techniques of negative painting.

**Raw materials**
Although we do not have detailed studies of the sources of clay available in antiquity, most of the coastal and highland valleys have clays suitable for potting. Clay occurs naturally in various locations such as the banks of ponds or in deeper deposits from which it can be dug as needed. It could have been transported to the workshops in panniers slung over the backs of llamas: modern Peruvian potters transport their clay, usually from sources up to 3 miles (5 km) away, in sacks slung across the backs of donkeys. Potters from the highlands sometimes travel with their clay down to the coast and make pots to order in the communities they visit. Today this practice seems to be confined to north Peru.

All raw clays generally contain some naturally occurring non-plastics (termed tempers by archaeologists) and this has certainly been found in the modern clays used by Quinua potters near Ayacucho. However, examination of ancient ceramics has shown that various non-plastics like crushed potsherds, pieces of shell and various grades of sand were used. The purpose of the non-plastics is to make the clay more workable and less liable to shrink and to facilitate the drying process so that it does not crack during the firing. Gerásimo Sosa, a modern artistic potter of Chulucanas, suggests the use of fine sand as a non-plastic, if it is required, for small ornamental pottery, while coarser sand is reserved for large utility vessels. Fine sand is plentiful, especially in the dunes of the coastal desert, while coarse sand can be found at a depth of about half a metre on parts of the north coast.

**27.** Large pot or *tinajón* full of sand for adding as a non-plastic in a workshop in Chulucanas in 1984. (Photograph: George Bankes.)

## Preparing the clay

*Soaking and adding non-plastics.* Information on the preparation of clay can be obtained by looking at the work of modern Peruvian potters like Gerásimo Sosa. He explains that the clay has first to be soaked. This can be done by piling it up like a volcano with a crater-like hole in the middle for water. Ideally, the proportion of water to dry clay should not exceed 40 per cent at the start of the process. The wet clay is dug out of the hole and dry clay is inserted in its place until all the clay has been soaked. Gerásimo's father said that in the old days (probably in his youth, in the first quarter of the twentieth century) potters in Simbilá used to sieve the clay through a sort of moistened hammock to free it of impurities.

Once the clay has been soaked Gerásimo says that clean sand can be added, roughly in a proportion of about 30 per cent or as needed, to act as a non-plastic. The next stage is to spread the clay, using hands or a shovel, on a piece of clean sacking. Some potters just use a clean floor with a layer of sand on top to separate the clay from the floor. The clay is piled up in the middle of the cloth and sprinkled by hand with water.

**28.** Treading clay in Morrope, showing the outer edge of the right foot being used for kneading. To the right of the treading cloth are two sacks containing the rest of the clay that was brought by donkey from about 3 miles (5 km) away. (Photograph: George Bankes, 1984.)

**29.** Pottery workshop near Morrope in 1984. The man on the right is preparing lumps of trodden clay (stacked on his left). His brother (centre) then rolls and beats the lumps into flat cakes (*tortillas*) that are then stacked on his right. (Photograph: George Bankes.)

**30.** Rolling out a *bolo* (skittle) of clay in Chulucanas in 1984. This forms the raw material for the initial hand-shaped chambers seen on the upper right. (Photograph: George Bankes.)

*Kneading.* The next stage is to tread the clay with bare feet, starting at the edge. The potter rests on his left foot and presses down with his right, using the outer edge of his foot. He starts from the edge and works round until he reaches the centre so that the clay is trodden over the whole cloth. Then the clay is picked up by hand, placed in the centre of the cloth, and the process is repeated. It is hard work and preferable to tread with both feet. In Morrope this process is called 'the dance'.

Once the clay is semi-kneaded it can be turned over, using the hands like spades to cut it up, so that the most kneaded part is at the bottom. Then the treading process is resumed. Water is added as necessary. Turning over the clay can be repeated up to three times and the process can last four hours or more.

When the kneading is finished the clay can be piled up. Then chunks can be cut out and rolled into flat cakes (called *bolos* in Chulucanas and *tortas* or *tortillas* in Morrope) which vary according to the size of the pot needed.

Preparation techniques like those just described for modern

potters in the Piura and Lambayeque Departments of north Peru are probably very similar to those employed in antiquity. Potting methods have been handed down within families from one generation to another. Gerásimo learnt his basic technique from his father, who would have learnt from his father when he was a boy in Simbilá and so on.

*Shaping.* The main methods of shaping pottery in pre-Hispanic Peru were modelling, coiling, moulding, and paddle and anvil. These are still used in the 1980s. The true potter's pivoted kick-wheel, like that used in medieval Europe, was unknown in pre-Hispanic Peru. However, between 1969 and 1973 about seventy fine-ware pedestal cups in the Recuay style were excavated at Pashash in the northern highlands. These cups had spin marks on their bases which suggested that they could have been made on a shaft-centred potter's wheel, but no such wheel has ever been found. In antiquity simple fired clay turntable discs were used. The earliest known example is from Paracas on the south coast dating to about 300 BC. In modern Peru these discs are mainly used in the highlands from the Callejón de Huaylas in the north to Lake Titicaca in the south. Often they are called *moldes* and are pottery supports used on a stone slab for rotating

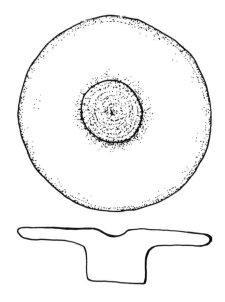

**31.** *Molde* or pottery support used in Raqch'i, Department of Cuzco, on a stone slab for rotating coil-built vessels while they are being made. (After Chavez, Karen Lynne Mohr, 'Traditional Pottery of Raqch'i, Cuzco, Peru: A Preliminary Study of Its Production, Distribution and Consumption' in *Ñawpa Pacha*, 22-3, figure 16.)

**32.** (Left) Moche effigy vessel with modelled ears and a puma held in the left hand. Height 260 mm. (Manchester Museum, 0.9707/2.)

**33.** (Right) A Morrope potter squeezing a coil of clay on to the top of a *tinaja*, 1984. He will smooth this coil with his hands and a damp cloth to form the neck. (Photograph: George Bankes.)

coil-built vessels while they are being made. There are large and small sizes with large ones having pedestal bases. At Machaqmarka, between Cuzco and Sicuani, the discs are called *pocos* and have a flat upper part with a short flaring cylinder underneath. *Pocos* range from 10 to 30 cm in diameter and are no more than 2 or 3 cm high. Potters still use more than one shaping method. For example, the chamber of a jar may be made by paddle and anvil while the neck is put on by coiling.

*Modelling* or direct shaping is simply working a lump of clay into the desired shape by hand. The Vicús potters who worked in the Chulucanas area during the second half of the first millennium BC made extensive use of modelling as a primary technique. Some idea of their method may be gleaned from the work of a modern Chulucanas potter like Gerásimo Sosa who has studied Vicús ceramics.

Gerásimo Sosa recommends starting off with at least half of the well prepared clay to be used. As a working surface he uses a table or a plaster floor, since the latter is porous. If he is making a bird he begins with its stomach and extends up the vertebral column to the head, beak and wings, using the thumb and middle finger to draw out the clay. When no more clay can be raised like this, coils are added to finish off. Once the upper body of a bird is finished the whole model is turned upside down with the tail being supported by a lump of clay. The bottom of the stomach and the feet can then be added. He emphasises that it is very important that the parts already completed do not dry out too much, and this can be prevented by covering with plastic bags. Periodically the fingers have to be moistened.

Moche potters used modelling as a secondary technique on mould-made vessels. This could consist of shaping the clay that is added to an object, such as a handle or the ears and earspools of a portrait vessel. Another method was to reshape the clay that was already part of a vessel and model a low relief face on a jar neck, for example. These techniques were used on certain types of vessel, notably jars, elaborate stirrup spout bottles, double-chambered whistling bottles, spout and handle bottles and

**34.** Nasca cup bowl made by coiling. The coils have been smoothed out but the rim is slightly irregular. Height 90 mm. (Manchester Museum, 0.7910.)

**35.** (Left) Fired clay mould for making a figurine, probably from the Ica/Chincha area. Height 108 mm. (Right) Reversed negative showing the figurine that would be produced from the mould on the left. (Manchester Museum, 0.4030/1.)

cooking pots. The whistling mechanisms of whistles were also made by modelling.

*Coiling* consists of rolling clay into a 'sausage' which is then wound round and pinched on to the wall of the vessel. It is often associated with another technique such as modelling or moulding. The earliest Initial Period plainware pottery, Guañape black plain, found in the Virú Valley, was made by hand-modelling, with the walls, especially around the rim, built up with coils. In the Early Intermediate Period Moche potters used coiling in conjunction with moulding. Experiments by Christopher Donnan on the manufacture of Moche ceramics have shown how coiling was used to finish off the chamber of a stirrup spout bottle that had been made in a two-piece mould. Coils of clay were applied by the Moche to stirrup spouts where they join the chamber.

Coiling was used extensively to make Nasca pottery.

*Moulding* comes into use in Peru from the Early Intermediate Period onwards, particularly by the Moche, Chimu and Chancay potters. Most Moche pottery objects were mould-made although not many moulds seem to have been placed in tombs. Moulds were made from fired clay that had been formed over an existing object such as a plant, an ear of maize or an existing pot. It is easy to make a mould by pressing clay round the chamber of a jar or stirrup spout bottle, cutting the clay in two and then removing the two halves as it begins to dry. Donnan's experiments have shown that moulding involved simply pressing moist clay into moulds. The clay would shrink away from the inside of the mould as it began to dry and could easily be removed. Donnan points out that there is no need to treat the inside of the mould artificially to remove the clay.

Two-piece moulds were the type most frequently used by the

**36.** Moche III stirrup spout bottle with an identical deer design (left) on each side and a flattened ridge (right) concealing the join of the two sections made in a two-piece mould. Height 240 mm. (Manchester Museum, 0.9707/27.)

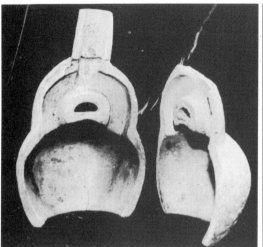 

37. (Left) Fired clay mould for a stirrup spout bottle (probably Chimu). (Brüning Archaeological Museum, Lambayeque.)

38. (Right) Fired clay stamp for making an impression of a feline. Probably Chancay; height 46 mm. (Manchester Museum, 0.4030/2.)

Moche and Chimu. If a pot was too complicated to be made in an ordinary two-piece mould it could be made in sections that could be joined together later. The Moche usually made the chambers of stirrup spout, spout and handle and whistling bottle forms in two-piece moulds as well as jars and dippers. Donnan also suggests that the mouths of Moche jars and dippers and various forms of heads, figures and other small objects added for ornamentation could have been made with two-piece moulds. Two-piece moulds for making complete stirrup spout bottles and jars have been found for Chimu ceramics in the Lambayeque area. After removal from the moulds the two sections of a Chimu pot were joined and this could have been helped by applying a thin clay wash much as modern potters do. This would leave a low seam along the junction, which could be removed by smoothing.

One-piece moulds were not often used for Moche pottery. They were employed to make figurines, the backs of which were hand-modelled and smoothed off. Donnan also suggests that they could have been used for the chambers of some stirrup spout bottles where the design involved fine detail. Those chambers which have a distinct ridge at the join could have been made from two halves each made in the same one-piece mould. When the two sections were joined it was probably necessary to have a thickened ridge to bind them together. Where a two-piece mould was used the two sections could be held together while still in the mould and it would have been easier to join them without an obvious ridge.

Chancay potters also used moulds extensively. Two-piece moulds for making the typical figurines with outstretched arms have been found. Some type of cord could have been used to hold the two sections of a mould together until the pressed clay inside had shrunk away a little from the sides.

*Paddle and anvil.* This technique involves raising the walls of a vessel by beating it on the outside with a wooden paddle while holding a round or oval stone inside to deaden the blows. Round

**39.** (Left) Wooden paddle stamp, probably pre-Hispanic; length 240 mm. (Right) Pottery stamp, probably pre-Hispanic; length 115 mm. (Brüning Museum, Lambayeque, 6180 and 108.)

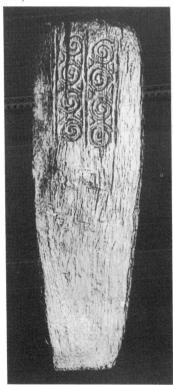

stones are used for vessels with globular or spherical chambers and oval ones for those with elongated forms. The origins of this method seem to go back to the early centuries AD in the Piura area, where it was used on some of the larger Vicús vessels. The technique of paddle stamping, which involves beating the still damp clay with a wooden paddle that has incised designs cut into it, may have developed after paddle and anvil had been going for some time. In the Lambayeque area paddle stamping was being used on utility vessels as early as AD 800 to 900. Further south, in the Trujillo area, paddle stamping first appears on Chimu ceramics about AD 1100.

Today paddle and anvil is used as a forming technique especially in the Departments of Lambayeque and Piura. In Morrope, modern paddle and anvil potters make utility vessels in several stages, usually working in the shade. Many potters use a convex mould to help shape the chamber. To make a *tinaja* or large jar, the previously prepared clay cake or *torta* and the mould are first dusted with dry powdered clay that acts as a separator. The *torta* is then slapped on to the mould and beaten down with the hands, moving anticlockwise round the mould. This initial form is enlarged by beating with a wide paddle, or *palmeta*, which is kept moistened. Then, after drying overnight, the chamber is finished by being upended and the walls are raised with a thick paddle or *mazo* while an anvil stone is held inside. The paddle is kept moistened. Alternatively the initial shaping is done entirely by hand and then the walls of the vessel are just raised by paddle and anvil, working anticlockwise round the workpiece. Necks are put on by adding a roll of clay, which is squeezed on and finally smoothed off with a damp cloth. Further rolls are added if a taller neck is needed.

In Simbilá and Chulucanas no moulds are used and many potters work sitting on a sack on the floor. Gerásimo Sosa has described the three main stages of making large vessels. The *bolo* of clay is first banged down on a cloth and pummelled by hand to make it cone-shaped. Then the potter, still seated, upends the vessel, places it on the lower part of his legs and beats the side with his right hand, turning the pot as necessary. The mouth is left wider than the base to avoid cracking. The second stage begins after these initial forms have been left to dry overnight. The potter sits down, puts the vessel between his legs and beats on the outside with a thinning paddle, deadening the blows by holding the anvil stone inside, rotating the pot all the time. Then the polishing paddle is used to smooth out the roughness. The

**40.** (Left) Paddling a *tinaja* chamber with a *mazo* in Morrope in 1984. The potter holds the anvil stone inside to deaden the blows and walks anticlockwise round his work. (Photograph: George Bankes.)

**41.** (Right) Initial forming of a vessel chamber using both hands to beat it out. This Chulucanas potter started from a *bolo* (figure 30) and is seated on the ground like most Chulucanas and Simbilá potters, 1984. (Photograph: George Bankes.)

paddles have to be kept wet. The walls are left thick for the third stage and the pots are set out in rows in the shade and covered with sacking. The third stage is raising. The potter sits or kneels down with legs apart and the vessel slightly inclined to the left. The walls are raised, using first the thinning and then the polishing paddles. The pot is lifted round as required. This work can also be done standing up, using a pottery pipe, resting the pot on it and walking round it. Sosa says that the results are the same with both methods but that constant kneeling while working can lead to rheumatism. Finally, necks are put on by adding rolls of clay as required in the same way as in Morrope.

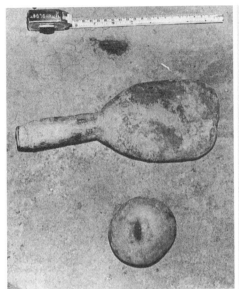

**42.** (Left) Paddle (top) and anvil stone (bottom) used by Gerásimo Sosa in Chulucanas in 1984. (Photograph: George Bankes.)

**43.** (Right) Moche III jar with a stamped design of three identical birds on the exterior. Height 260 mm. (Manchester Museum, 0.9707/1.)

*Stamping.* This method of ornamentation was used particularly by Moche potters. Paddle stamping was also employed on the north coast and is still in use in areas of paddle and anvil working.

Stamps have always been made of fired clay formed over actual objects like sea shells or ears of corn or fired clay matrices. When made over clay matrices stamps generally represent human or animal forms. On Moche pots only one type of stamp would be used on a single vessel. Stamps were arranged symmetrically so that on a spherical jar they would be evenly distributed.

According to Donnan's experiments the most common method of stamping used by the Moche was to place the stamp against the outside of the vessel while the clay was still malleable. Then the potter could reach inside the piece and push the side out into the stamp. When the stamp was removed a relief impression would be left on the vessel wall. The other method involved pressing moist clay into the stamp, which was then pressed against the outside of the vessel. The stamp was then removed, leaving the clay inside it sticking to the vessel wall. This had the advantage of not having to reach inside the pot, but Donnan found it difficult to make the clay stick to the wall and air pockets could form in the clay. Relatively few Moche pots seem to have been stamped in this way.

Paddle stamping involves beating the outside of a vessel with a wooden or pottery stamp incised with a design. Two examples of pre-Hispanic stamps are known from the Lambayeque area. Today some of the paddle and anvil potters of Morrope and Simbilá use fired clay stamps, which are usually oval with geometric and floral designs. The stamping is generally done in a single horizontal line on the upper part of the chamber of a vessel before the neck is put on.

### Finishing

*Smoothing.* Once the shape of a vessel was complete the surface would most likely need to be smoothed to remove the ripples left from the building process. In antiquity the surface of vessels could have been abraded, first by using items like maize cobs, pieces of bone, stones, mussel shells and pieces of gourd. Then cloth or leather could have been used to rub the surface.

*Painting.* In pre-Hispanic Peru slips and mineral pigments were used extensively to decorate pottery. The earliest paints used

**44.** Set of fired clay stamps used by a female Morrope potter in 1984. (Photograph: George Bankes.)

**45.** (Left) Vase with a painted design in purple, orange, black, cream and white of a mythical bird, usually termed the 'Horrible Bird', eating a trophy head. Middle Nasca, phase 5, height 105 mm. (Manchester Museum, 0.8100/1.)

**46.** (Right) Moche III face-neck jar. The upper part of the right arm outlined in fugitive black paint emerges from the white slip band round the wrist. Height 235 mm. (Manchester Museum, 0.9707/25.)

were probably the red, white and yellow pigments that were applied to incised lines on Waira-jirca pottery in the second millennium BC. In south Peru, in the first millennium BC, incised designs were coloured after firing with mineral pigments mixed with resins forming a lacquer-like coating.

On the south coast Nasca potters excelled in the use of mineral paints which were probably prepared by grinding and wetting and then mixing with a clay slip (a suspension of fine clay in water). In his study of Nasca pottery, Donald Proulx has found between thirteen and fifteen distinct colours on some vessels dating to the middle period of the style. Colours ranged from black and white through purple, shades of red and orange, yellow, grey, brown, violet and pink. These colours occur in both the Ica and Nazca valleys, but the frequency of use varies considerably and in Ica pink is used only as a background while in Nazca it occurs in designs. The quality of paint varies and the white used in Ica is poorer than that used on vessels of the same age in Nazca. Also there are temporal differences in pigments, with the earlier ones being thicker than the later ones.

Some research has been done on possible origins for Nasca mineral pigments in the Ica Valley. Haematite (iron ore) has been suggested as a source for red, while limonite, a hydrated haematite, was probably used to produce yellow. Pyrolusite (magnesium dioxide) is a possible source for black. Mixing these powdered minerals could produce different colours so that dark brown resulted from mixing pyrolusite with haematite. White clay slip could have formed the white background. The painting on Nasca pottery seems to have been accomplished according to strict rules for design layout and method of portrayal as, for example, in the depiction of mythical beings. There were also rules about background colour so that only certain colours like white, black, red, orange and pink were used for this.

In contrast to Nasca, Moche potters used only two basic colours of slip pigment, red and white. A very pure white clay was used to make the white slip. Red pigments seem to have been made from a clay similar to that used to make the pots but of a finer texture and without impurities. In addition, a fugitive black

**47.** Moche III jar of an anthropomorphised head with owl eyes and nose and feline fangs. The facial features are emphasised by white slip on a red background. Height 155 mm. (Manchester Museum, 0.9707/3.)

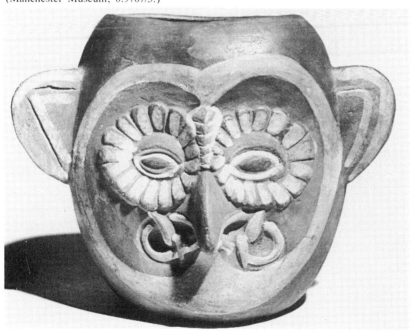

**48.** Collared bowl with a negative painted spot and double zigzag design. Made by the Arabela Group, River Curaray, north-east Peru, c.1985; height 83 mm. (Manchester Museum, 0.9736.)

**49.** Early Nasca bowl with a high degree of interior polishing, emphasising the fish design, while the plain exterior is left unpolished. Width 230 mm. (Manchester Museum, 0.9707/56.)

organic pigment was painted on to many vessels after firing. According to Donnan, the pots were then heated to scorch the substance on to the surface. This black was applied only to vessels painted with the other two colours and was most frequently used in the Virú Valley.

Where they used just red and white, Moche potters seem to have wanted to achieve a contrast between the two colours, which were flat, without any deliberate attempt at shading. Often part of the outer surface of a vessel would be left unpainted but was later polished with the pigmented areas. This would result in two shades of red, since the colour of the clay from which the pot was made would be different from that of the pigment. Shades of red and white also reflected how much polishing had been done and the firing conditions. In addition, differences in the pigments led to differences in colour.

Negative painting may well have started originally simply as black smudging surrounding the natural colour of the clay as a result of firing in a primitive wood kiln. Modern negative painted pottery made by Gerásimo Sosa involves drawing out the required designs on the polished surface of the pot using a substance impervious to heat, like damp clay, which is put on just before the second firing. After firing the clay cover is removed, leaving a light colour underneath, while the rest is reduced to black, with some areas darker than others, so that each pot has its unique colouring.

*Polishing.* Glazes were not used in pre-Hispanic Peru, so polishing or rubbing the surface before firing to give it a shine was the main way of obtaining a glossy finish. A fine hard stone would have been used to polish the still damp clay vessel, and Gerásimo Sosa says that this process seals the porous clay and produces a shine that becomes opaque as the vessel dries. In consequence, a second polishing is necessary to restore the shine. Gerásimo adds that the water in the clay acts as a lubricant so that the stone will rub. Furthermore, he points out that initially one can polish from one side to another but to finish off it is best to follow one direction — such as left to right or up and down — to improve the polishing marks. Donnan points out that rubbing the vessel with the hand or a soft cloth while polishing will help remove stroke marks.

On Moche pottery usually only the painted areas were polished. On Nasca ceramics the design area is always the most carefully polished. The bottoms and interiors of exterior-painted

**50.** *Tinajas* drying in Morrope alongside a *cenicero* of smoking goat's dung, 1984. The temperature of the dung can reach 550 C. (Photograph: George Bankes.)

Nasca vessels have only minimal polishing. Proulx found that polishing had sometimes smudged the colours and, in consequence, blurred the designs. The high sheen that can be seen on some polychrome pots is sometimes the result of waxing by modern owners.

*Preparation for firing.* In pre-Hispanic and modern Peru the drying of pottery is an essential stage before firing, since any damp retained in the clay will lead to its cracking. The huge quantities of pre-Hispanic pottery from the coast have been partly attributed to the climate, which is drier and sunnier than the highlands and allows a large number of ceramics to be sun-dried before firing. This process also allows defects to be patched with clay. Modern Simbilá potters put their pieces out to dry early in the morning of a sunny day. Also during the morning utility vessels are covered with a thin wash made from iron oxide powder and water which dries yellow and turns red after firing. By late afternoon the pots will be dry, having been turned from time to time so that they dry evenly. In Morrope, the drying process for larger utility vessels is helped by placing them along

**51.** Kiln in Simbilá packed ready for firing, with its covering of straw and dung, 1984. In the foreground is a firing hole, while to the right is a wind-break of sacking supported by wooden stakes. (Photograph: George Bankes.)

**52.** Partially unpacked kiln in Chulucanas showing a layer of upright *tinajones* (one cracked) on the bottom with *tinajas* laid horizontally above, 1984. Remains of the covering of sherds along with ash from the burnt straw and dung can be seen on top of the *tinajas*. (Photograph: George Bankes.)

either side of a 6 metre long *cenicero* (ash tray) of smoking goat dung, which can reach a temperature of 550 C.

*Firing*. The evidence to date for pre-Hispanic firing methods is sparse. At Galindo in the Moche Valley remains of a ceramic workshop included a floor covered with burnt ash and manure. At Batan Grande in the Lambayeque Valley there is some evidence for a closed ceramic kiln: it is likely that reduction-fired blackware ceramics would have been made in closed kilns that excluded oxygen. The methods used to make oxidised wares in pre-Hispanic times were probably similar to those used in the 1970s and 1980s to make utility wares in open-pit kilns on the north coast and in the 'bonfires' of the highlands.

The preferred fuel of modern Simbilá and Chulucanas potters is the wood of the *zapote*, which gives a good steady heat, with temperatures up to 950 C. *Algarrobo* wood is used in Morrope, but its higher temperature, up to 1100 C, is offset by its more rapid heating and cooling, which can lead to cracking.

The firing pits of the north coast are about 30 to 50 cm deep by about 4 to 6 metres across. The fuel is laid on the bottom and then the largest pots are carefully set base down in the wood, which is then packed between them to keep them rigid. Next, a layer of similar-sized vessels is laid horizontally across the top and smaller pots are set above that. Great care is taken so that every piece is firmly in place, since any slippage during firing could lead to breakages. Between eighty and a hundred vessels, depending on size, can go into one firing. When all the pottery is packed a layer of sherds is placed over the whole mound, leaving about three small holes to ignite the fire. A layer of straw and animal dung is strewn on top. A wind-break of stakes or sacking is often erected on the side of the prevailing wind. The kiln is lit at the fire holes, which are then covered. Firing usually starts on a Saturday afternoon and takes about twelve hours.

In the highlands the 'bonfire' technique is similar to that used for the north coast pit-kilns. At Machaqmarka, in the south highlands, a kiln used in the early 1970s had a stone base about half a metre high which was covered with a layer of dried wood and cow dung when used for firing. Dried grass was also used in firing. The kiln was fired for about two to three hours.

These modern firing methods produce few breakages but rely on fine weather with little wind. If there is damp nothing can be fired.

# 4
# Iconography of pre-Hispanic pottery

In pre-Hispanic Peru, especially on the coast, there were two categories of ceramics: utility vessels and fancy decorated pots. These two classes were not exclusive and the Inca, for example, used aryballoid jars with painted designs for liquids. The meaning of the designs on pre-Hispanic Peruvian pottery is still a matter of debate among archaeologists and art historians. Since none of the potters or their contemporaries could write about the content of their art there is only the evidence of archaeology and the actual designs. Spanish accounts at the time of the conquest make very few references to pottery since their main concern was with precious metals.

The most thorough method of studying the iconography is to build up a large photographic reference collection of one style and try to discern themes. This has been done for Moche ceramics by Christopher Donnan and a similar study is under way for Nasca. The design themes on pottery are not exclusive to that medium and relate also to those on stone carvings, textiles and murals. Donnan has suggested that most Moche fancy pottery, like stirrup spout bottles, was for ritual use and certainly some of it can be seen in ceremonial scenes. However, fragments of these vessels have been found in domestic refuse, which suggests that they were kept in houses as well as being placed in tombs to accompany their former owners. The designs on pots can be regarded as representational and symbolic art forms which featured both everyday and mythical subjects.

## Chavín art

The most common motif of Chavín art is one in which the mouth of the creature is depicted as a snarling cat with teeth bared and long pointed canines projecting over the lips. The cat that the artists probably intended to represent is the jaguar, a legendary beast admired for its strength and courage throughout tropical America. The most complete feline figures in Chavín art have the pelage markings of jaguars. The cat appears in its natural context as well as in the mouths of human figures, snakes and birds. The use of the cat mouth has been suggested by John Rowe as an indicator of divine and mythological beings as opposed to ordinary natural creatures, implying a comparison between the power of the jaguar and that of nature. In this light

**53.** (Left) Moche Period *chicha olla* (with some restoration) from a tomb at Huanchaco, near Trujillo, *c.*AD 200-500. Height 730 mm. (Photograph: George Bankes.)

**54.** (Below) Two-handled dish. Inside are painted two catfish in dark red on orange. Probably made in the Lake Titicaca area, Inca; diameter 170 mm. (Manchester Museum, 0.9703/1.)

the cat could be considered as a sort of visual metaphor. Snakes also appear as appendages to anthropomorphic figures in Chavín art and these serpents, probably also derived from the tropical forest, have been interpreted as visual metaphors for hair. Other animals that feature in Chavín art include raptorial birds like eagles and reptiles like the cayman.

This feline motif continued in Cupisnique ceramics and a version also appeared on the south coast in the Paracas pottery of Ica. The north coast renderings were usually incised on polished grey or black wares. The Paracas versions were incised and painted, with the feline set on the end of the bottle instead of on its side as on the north coast.

### Felines on Moche and Chimu ceramics

By about 300 BC the Chavín-inspired feline motifs had died out. They reappeared on the north coast on some Moche III jars and stirrup spout bottles, on which they were incised and painted in the form of a cat with its mouth wide open. Fanged anthropomorphic figures with a mixture of human, bird or animal

**55.** Stirrup spout bottle. At the base of the stirrup handle are two eagle heads with feline mouths; the other two heads are human. From the Lambayeque Department, middle Cupisnique, height 228 mm. (Courtesy of the National Museums of Scotland, 1909.248.)

**56.** (Left) Spout and handle bottle with an incised feline face in the Paracas style derived from Chavín art. From the Upper Ica Valley, Juan Pablo I site; height 150 mm. (Courtesy of the Peabody Museum, Harvard University, 58-51-30/8170. Photograph: Hillel Burger.)

**57.** (Right) Moche IV stirrup-spout bottle with dark red painted design of a 'fish monster' with the fangs and tongue of a feline. Its hand holds a *tumi* (ceremonial knife). Height 280 mm. (Manchester Museum, 0.9707/11.)

attributes also appear in Moche III and IV, on modelled and painted pots. One phase III example has been found associated with fish and another has what looks like a starfish just in front of its mouth. It has, therefore, been suggested that this Moche feline is the head of a large fish, possibly of a mythical being. The Moche may well have misunderstood the felines which they saw on Cupisnique pots. A fish monster painted with human limbs and fish fins on a phase IV stirrup spout bottle has the large fangs and tongue that a feline would have.

Some Chimu blackware stirrup spout bottles have a grinning feline set on the side or the end. These probably represent a continuation of the tradition that stretched back to Chavín times. From Spanish accounts of Chimu religion the feline does not seem to have been a deity.

## Moche iconography

Donnan's extensive study of Moche ceramics has revealed some themes and canons in Moche art. The most obvious canon is the highly realistic nature of Moche art, with subject matter closely related to the immediate environment of Moche artists. The scale is small, with most designs being between 5 and 25 cm high so that nearly everything is shown smaller than life size. Frequently more than one figure is shown on a design, but natural scales are used for people and animals. Anthropomorphised figures with human and animal attributes are generally depicted at human scale.

Moche artists observed conventions indicating pose and action for anthropomorphic and human figures. The distance between the feet indicated whether figures were standing, walking, running or dancing. The position of the torso was varied to show speed, falling or death. Running figures are shown with the body tilted forward, while dead ones can be shown horizontal, upside down or with splayed arms and legs.

Attempts have been made to distinguish the work of individual potters but this is difficult since none signed their work. Donnan has pointed out that even though many pots have identical forms they are not necessarily by the same artist, since duplicate moulds were probably available. Different potters could share a set of

**58.** Moche IV fine line painting showing prisoners stripped naked. The spread-eagled figure on the left is dead, while those carrying the people in the litters are running. (After Donnan, Christopher B., *Moche Art and Iconography*, figure 15.)

**59.** Two portrait jars of figures chewing coca leaves while holding a lime gourd and a spatula, most likely made by the same potter. Moche III; height 213 mm. (Courtesy of the Lowie Museum of Anthropology, University of California at Berkeley, 4-2963 and 4-2964.)

moulds to produce pieces identical in form. If two identical pots, made and finished in exactly the same way, are found in the same tomb then they may be by the same artist. Fine line painting in red and white slip can reveal more closely the work of a single artist. For example, examination in detail of the depiction of the chin, nose, mouth and leg of an anthropomorphised bean-runner has been suggested by Donnan as indicating whether or not similar paintings were done by the same artist.

## Themes on ancient Peruvian pottery

Studies suggest that a limited number of themes feature on

**60.** (Left) Portrait jar of a seated person offering a goblet. Chancay; height 400 mm. (Manchester Museum, 0.9707/52.)

**61.** (Below) Bowl showing a mythical being wearing a mouth-mask and head ornament. The hand under the chin is clutching a trophy head. Middle Nasca, phase 5; height 95 mm. (Manchester Museum, 0.8123.)

ancient Peruvian ceramics. On fine line-painted Moche pottery a 'presentation theme' has been perceived as a major one by Donnan. This involves the presentation of a goblet to a rayed figure, wearing a conical helmet and a short skirt and shirt, as part of an elaborate ceremony. A much more simplified version is found on Chancay portrait jars, where a seated person is shown offering a goblet, but we do not know for whom it is intended. Moche pottery also illustrates the offering of cloth. Certainly wool cloth and cotton cloth were important as tribute items in the Inca Empire and there is archaeological evidence for their importance before then.

On Nasca ceramics the polychrome designs feature many

62. Modern fake of an anthropomorphic jar in Middle Horizon style. The design on the poncho is completely at variance with the conventions of Middle Horizon textiles. Height 170 mm. (Manchester Museum, 0.9707/63.)

**63.** Copy of a Middle Horizon Atarco-style urn almost certainly made by the 'Wari Forger', probably in the 1920s. Height 230 mm. (Manchester Museum, 0.9707/69.)

variations on the theme of an anthropomorphic mythical being in the form of a semi-human masked creature, often shown clutching a human trophy head. This appears especially on double spout and bridge bottles. All have a distinctive mouth-mask and forehead ornament which have been found made of gold in some of the richer Nasca tombs. This has prompted the suggestion that these masked creatures could represent masked dancers.

### Misreconstructions and forgeries

During the twentieth century there have been misreconstructions and forgeries of both mould-made and slip-decorated pre-Hispanic ceramics from Peru. This process can involve either the restoration of broken pottery smashed by grave robbers or the reproduction of ancient pieces, which are then passed off as genuine antiquities. The earliest forgeries were probably of Moche and Chimu pottery in the nineteenth century. After the German archaeologist Uhle excavated Nasca graves in 1901 there was intensive looting of south coast cemeteries to satisfy the demand from foreign museums. Many pots got broken or damaged and had to be restored to make them salable. Restoration at the beginning of the twentieth century often involved mending broken pottery with thick shellac as an adhesive, then smoothing down ill fitting joints with sandpaper. Finally, designs that were very different from the original iconography were put on with oil-based paints.

During the 1920s and 1930s polychrome painted pottery (then termed 'Coast Tiahuanaco', now called Wari) was found at Pachacamac, Ocucaje and Pacheco. This created a demand from museums and private collectors. A skilled forger, termed the 'Wari Forger' by Alan Sawyer, helped supply this market. Although he made use of some ancient pots, on such items as ponchos he painted designs which were far more elaborate than those on genuine Wari pieces. The forgeries of this potter became apparent only after research on designs on Wari ceramics was published in the 1960s, and the first publication exposing his work was by Sawyer in 1982.

# 5
# Modern Peruvian pottery

In the 1980s both utility and ornamental pottery are being produced on the coast, in the highlands and in the tropical forest of Peru. Much of this is made with pre-Hispanic techniques like coiling, moulding and paddle and anvil, but some potters have adopted the European-style potters' kick-wheel. For example, until the early 1980s Morrope potters exclusively used the paddle and anvil technique. Then a potter from Cajamarca (in the highlands about 100 miles [160 km] south-east as the crow flies) demonstrated a kick-wheel and tried to set up a pottery centre in Morrope. Most of the Morrope potters preferred their paddle and anvil method but four young ones took up the wheel. However, these four insisted on using the wheels at home in their own workshops and not in the now empty craft centre. During a study tour of potting communities in 1972 an American pottery teacher, Gertrude Litto, found that in only one of them, Pucará, was the kick-wheel in general use, in spite of over four hundred years of European influence.

Utility pottery is mainly produced for cooking, storage and the manufacture, serving and storage of *chicha*. The nomenclature is largely Spanish, particularly on the coast, so that a general-purpose cooking pot is an *olla* while a jug is a *jarra*. On the north coast the pre-Hispanic Quechua term *callana*, meaning 'cooking pot', is used for a bowl in Morrope and, more widely, for the sherds used to cover pit-kilns that have been packed ready for firing. There is an element of male/female duality in the names for some vessels and this may have pre-Hispanic roots. In Simbilá there are pots with names that indicate that they have a masculine sex or characteristics, like the *cántaro* (jar), *corbatón* (jar with a tie) or *muco* (round-based jar with lugs). Feminine Simbilá vessels include the *cantarilla* (flask), *tinaja tetona* (jar with two teats) and the *chicha olla* (pot for boiling *chicha*). Some forms, especially the varieties of jugs, have been derived from Spanish prototypes. However, other shapes like the *chicha olla* and *cantarilla* seem to be directly descended from pre-Hispanic forms. The *tostadoras* (toasting pots for maize and coffee) that can be bought in the Cuzco market probably have their origins in a similar form discovered at the Inca city of Machu Picchu. Glazes are rarely used on this utility pottery and most examples are from the highlands and are decorated with lead glazes, especially those from Pucará. Indigenous clay slips and washes are preferred for painted decoration.

### Sañoc Camayoc

Sañoc Camayoc (a Spanish version of the Quechua *Sanuq-Kamayoq*, meaning 'pottery specialists') is a group of young artistic potters who established themselves in Chulucanas in 1975. Its principal members are Gerásimo Sosa Alache, his cousin Flavio Sosa Maza and Segundo Moncada, Gerásimo's brother-in-law. Gerásimo, like many Peruvian potters, learned the techniques, particularly of paddle and anvil working, from his father. His father was born in Simbilá, where he used to work making utility wares until he emigrated from there to Chulucanas. Gerásimo used to make what he terms *alfarería* (utility pottery) but now makes only *cerámica* (fine pottery), since he did not find making the same forms of utility pots, like *tinajas* and *chicha ollas*, day after day very satisfying. In the late 1970s he, Flavio and Segundo started studying Vicús ceramics, which were originally discovered near Chulucanas in the 1960s by tomb robbers. They experimented with production techniques, particularly with negative painting. They received assistance and

**64.** Cooking *ollas* (centre and foreground) and bowls (upper left) in La Unión market, Department of Piura, 1984. (Photograph: George Bankes.)

**65.** *Olla* for cooking *chicha*. Made by paddle and anvil with a coiled rim in 1984 by Santos Raymundo Lopez of Simbilá. Height 400 mm. (Manchester Museum, 0.9726/22.)

**66.** Figure vessel decorated with a negative painted dot and line design, depicting a kneeling woman. Made in 1984 by Flavio Sosa of Chulucanas. Height 175 mm. (Manchester Museum, 0.9726/32.)

encouragement from various outsiders like Gloria Joyce, an American Catholic missionary sister, and Lupe Camino, a Peruvian ceramics teacher. After the heavy rains of 1983 the Centro de Investigación y Promoción del Campesinado of Piura provided assistance to Gerásimo in reconstructing his workshop. Gerásimo also gives pottery classes.

Only fine clay without any sand mixed in with it is used to make the ornamental pots of Sañoc Camayoc. Hand modelling, paddle and anvil, coiling, polishing with a smooth stone and negative painting are the main methods used. Closed kilns are now employed and Gerásimo fires at between 600 and 800 C.

**67.** Tripartite vessel of a *chichera* with two *tinajas* with negative painted geometric designs. Made in 1986 by Gerásimo Sosa of Chulucanas. Height 290 mm. (Manchester Museum, 0.9707/39.)

Whistling vessels in the form of birds are also made. Certain themes run through their work and these range from geometric designs to indigenous figures from Chulucanas and the surrounding area. One particular subject of Gerásimo's is the *chichera*, the lady who makes *chicha*. His early examples (about 1980) on this theme consist of a tripartite vessel with a lady in front of whom are two *tinajas*. He then made examples of a fatter *chichera*, seated, with *tinajas* and *cantaros* ranged in a line round her. A 1986 *chichera* he made for the Manchester Museum is again a tripartite vessel, but the lady is fatter than her 1980 counterparts. Gerásimo freely admits that he prefers to create new things since life is more interesting that way. As a result there is much variety in his work and each piece is unique.

In spite of his closed kiln Gerásimo is not immune from the effects of the weather. In 1986, when he started on the Manchester *chichera*, the first piece he made cracked during firing because it rained on that particular day. Making such tripartite vessels is difficult, since each section has to rest level with the others to avoid straining the joins. All the members of

Sañoc Camayoc sign and date their work, usually on the base, by incising the clay before it is fired. The principal outlet for the wares of this group is through a gallery in Lima called Antisuyu, where the buyers are mainly foreigners and rich Peruvians.

**Eduardo Calderón Palomino**
Eduardo Calderón Palomino is a shaman or healer who also makes fine pottery. He lives and works in Las Delicias, near the modern settlement of Moche. His subjects often feature the indigenous women of Moche performing various tasks like grinding corn or making a mat. His methods include modelling, moulding, polishing with the end of a ballpoint pen and painting with clay slips. His pieces are distinctive but lack the finish and inspiration of the work of Gerásimo Sosa. He also makes replicas of Moche pottery for sale to tourists. His original pieces are signed and dated by incising the clay on the base before firing.

**68.** Modelled and painted (white and two shades of brown) figure vessel of a woman using a grinding stone. Made in 1969 in Las Delicias, Moche, by Eduardo Calderón Palomino. Height 250 mm. (Private collection.)

# 6
# Museums

The museums listed here are the main ones known to contain Peruvian pottery. Intending visitors are advised to check opening times before making a special journey.

## United Kingdom
*Birmingham Museum and Art Gallery*, Chamberlain Square, Birmingham B3 3DH. Telephone: 021-235 2834.
*Bolton Museum and Art Gallery*, Le Mans Crescent, Bolton, Lancashire BL1 1SE. Telephone: 0204 22311, extension 2191.
*Brighton Art Gallery and Museum*, Church Street, Brighton, East Sussex. Telephone: 0273 603005.
*Cambridge University Museum of Archaeology and Anthropology*, Downing Street, Cambridge CB2 3DZ. Telephone: 0223 337733 or 333516.
*City of Bristol Museum and Art Gallery*, Queens Road, Bristol BS8 1RL. Telephone: 0272 299771.
*Horniman Museum*, London Road, Forest Hill, London SE23 3PQ. Telephone: 01-699 1872 or 2339 or 4911.
*Ipswich Museum*, High Street, Ipswich, Suffolk IP1 3QH. Telephone: 0473 213761-2.
*Liverpool Museum*, William Brown Street, Liverpool L3 8EN. Telephone: 051-207 0001 or 5451.
*Manchester Museum*, University of Manchester, Oxford Road, Manchester M13 9PL. Telephone: 061-273 3333.
*Museum of Mankind*, 6 Burlington Gardens, London W1X 2EX. Telephone: 01-323 8043.
*Pitt Rivers Museum*, South Parks Road, Oxford OX1 3PP. Telephone: 0865 270927.
*Royal Albert Memorial Museum*, Queen Street, Exeter, Devon EX4 3RX. Telephone: 0392 265858.
*Royal Museum of Scotland*, Chambers Street, Edinburgh EH1 1JF. Telephone: 031-225 7534.
*Ulster Museum*, Botanic Gardens, Belfast BT9 5AB. Telephone: 0232 381251-6.

## Austria
*Museum für Völkerkunde*, Heldenplatz 3, Neue Hofburg, 1010 Vienna 1.

**Belgium**
*Musées Royaux d'Art et d'Histoire*, Avenue J. F. Kennedy, 1040 Brussels.

**Denmark**
*Nationalmuseet*, Fredericksholms Kanal 12, 1220 Copenhagen.

**France**
*Musée de l'Homme*, Palais de Chaillot, Place du Trocadéro, 75016 Paris.

**Germany (West)**
*Linden Museum of Ethnology*, Hegelplatz 1, 7000 Stuttgart, Baden-Württemberg.
*Museum für Völkerkunde*, Arnimallee 23-27, 1000 Berlin 33.
*Roemer-Pelizaeus Museum*, Am Steine 1, 3200 Hildesheim, Niedersachsen.
*Staatliches Museum für Völkerkunde*, Maximilianstrasse 42, 8000 Munich 22, Bavaria.

**Holland**
*Rijksmuseum voor Volkenkunde*, Steenstraat 1, 2300 AE, Leiden, Zuid Holland.

**Italy**
*International Museum of Ceramics*, Via Campidori 1, 48018, Faenza.
*Museo Preistorico Etnografico Luigi Pigorini*, Via Lincoln 1, 00187, Rome.

**Peru**
*Archaeological Museum*, Calle Tigre 165, Cuzco.
*Archaeological Museum of Trujillo University*, Calle Bolivar 466, Trujillo.
*Brüning Archaeological Museum*, Calle 2 de Mayo 48, Lambayeque.
*Museo Nacional de Antropología y Arqueología*, Plaza Bolivar, Pueblo Libre, Lima.
*Rafael Larco Herrera Museum*, Avenida Bolivar 1515, Pueblo Libre, Lima.

**Spain**
*Museo de las Américas*, Avenida de los Reyes Catolicos, Ciudad Universitaria, Madrid 3.
*Museu Etnològic*, Paseo de Santa Madrona, Parque de Montjuic, 08004, Barcelona.

**United States of America**
*American Museum of Natural History*, 70th Street and Central Park West, New York, NY 10024.
*Metropolitan Museum of Art*, 5th Avenue at 82nd Street, New York, NY 10028.
*Peabody Museum of Archaeology and Ethnology*, 11 Divinity Avenue, Cambridge, Massachusetts 02138.
*Peabody Museum of Natural History*, Yale University, 170 Whitney Avenue, New Haven, Connecticut 06520.
*Robert H. Lowie Museum of Anthropology*, 103 Kroeber Hall, University of California, Berkeley, California 94720.
*Smithsonian Institution*, 100 Jefferson Drive SW, Washington DC 20560.

# 7
# Further reading

Most of these books are available only in the libraries of a few large museums and universities.

Arnold, Dean Edward. 'Native Pottery Making in Quinua, Peru', *Anthropos*, volume 67, 5 and 6, Freiburg, 39-47.

Bankes, George. *Moche Pottery from Peru*. British Museum, London, 1980.

Bankes, George. 'Paddle and Anvil Potters of the North Coast of Peru' in Nick Saunders and Olivier de Montmollin (editors), *Recent Studies in Pre-Columbian Archaeology*. British Archaeological Reports International Series, 421, 545-63, Oxford, 1988.

Bock, Edward K. de. *Moche: Gods, Warriors, Priests*. Leiden, 1988.

Burger, Richard L. *The Prehistoric Occupation of Chavín de Huántar, Peru*. University of California Publications in Anthropology, 14, Berkeley/Los Angeles, 1984.

Chavez, Karen Lynne Mohr. 'Traditional Pottery of Raqch'i, Cuzco, Peru: A Preliminary Study of Its Production, Consumption and Distribution', *Ñawpa Pacha*, 22-3, 161-224, Berkeley, California 1984-5.

Donnan, Christopher B. 'Moche Ceramic Technology', *Ñawpa Pacha*, 3, 115-36, Berkeley, California, 1965.

Donnan, Christopher B. *Moche Art and Iconography*. University of California, Los Angeles, 1976.

Donnan, Christopher B., and McClelland, Donna. *The Burial Theme in Moche Iconography*. Dumbarton Oaks, Washington DC, 1979.

Grieder, Terence. *The Art and Archaeology of Pashash*. University of Texas Press, Austin and London, 1978.

Lathrap, Donald W. *The Upper Amazon*. London, 1970.

Litto, Gertrude. *South American Folk Pottery*. Watson-Guptill Publications, New York, 1976.

Proulx, Donald A. *Local Differences and Time Differences in Nasca Pottery*. University of California Publications in Anthropology, volume 5, 1968.

Proulx, Donald A. 'The Nasca Style' in Lois Katz (editor), *Art of the Andes: Pre-Columbian Sculptures and Painted Ceramics from the Arthur M. Sackler Collections*, 87-105. Arthur M.

Sackler Foundation, Washington DC, 1983.
Rowe, John Howland. *Chavín Art: An Inquiry into Its Form and Meaning.* Museum of Primitive Art, New York, 1962.
Sawyer, Alan R. *Ancient Peruvian Ceramics. The Nathan Cummings Collection.* Metropolitan Museum of Art, New York, 1966.
Sawyer, Alan R. 'The Falsification of Ancient Peruvian Slip-decorated Ceramics' in Elizabeth H. Boone (editor), *Falsifications and Misreconstructions of Pre-Columbian Art.* Dumbarton Oaks, Washington DC, 1982.
Sosa, Gerásimo. *El Barro Nos Unío.* Centro de Investigación y Promoción del Campesinado, Piura, 1984.

# Index

Page numbers in italic refer to illustrations.